C000269360

THE COMPLETE ORDER OF CELEBRATING MATRIMONY

with Nuptial Mass and Readings

for use of congregations in
the dioceses of England and Wales

*All booklets are published thanks to the
generous support of the members of the
Catholic Truth Society*

CATHOLIC TRUTH SOCIETY
PUBLISHERS TO THE HOLY SEE

Contents

The Complete Order of Celebrating Matrimony © 2016 The Incorporated Catholic Truth Society, 40-46 Harleyford Road, London SE11 5AY Tel: 020 7640 0042 Fax: 020 7640 0046. The English translation and chants for the Order of Mass © 2010 International Commission on English in the Liturgy Corporation. All rights reserved. The English translation of the Order of Celebrating Matrimony © 2013 International Commission on English in the Liturgy Corporation. All rights reserved. The Civil Declaration of Freedom © 2013 Bishops' Conference of England and Wales. All rights reserved. The Scripture Readings are taken from the Jerusalem Bible, © 1966 Darton Longman & Todd and Doubleday & Company Inc. The Responsorial Psalms are taken from the Grail Psalter by permission of the Grail, England and W. Collins, Sons and Co Ltd. The Order of the Celebration of Matrimony was confirmed by the Congregation for Divine Worship and the Discipline of the Sacraments on 25 March 2015. Prot. No. 88/15

Concordat cum originali: Paul Moynihan

Imprimatur: ✠ Peter Smith, Archbishop of Southwark, 10 February 2016

The Introductory Rites

After the wedding guests have gathered in the church, the entrance of the bridal party may take one of two forms:

The First Form: At the appointed time, the Priest goes with the servers to the door of the church, receives the bridal party, and warmly greets them, showing that the Church shares in their joy.

The procession to the altar then takes place whilst the Entrance Chant (or a suitable hymn or song) is sung.

The Priest approaches the altar, reverences it with a profound bow, and venerates it with a kiss. After this, he goes to the chair.

The Second Form: At the appointed time, the Priest goes with the servers to the place prepared for the couple or to his chair.

When the couple have arrived at their place, the Priest receives them and warmly greets them, showing that the Church shares in their joy.

Then, during the Entrance Chant (or a suitable hymn or song), the Priest approaches the altar, reverences it with a profound bow, and venerates it with a kiss. After this, he goes to the chair.

Entrance Chant

A

Cf. Ps 19:3,5

May the Lord send you help from the holy place,
and give you support from Sion.
May he grant you your hearts' desire
and fulfil every one of your designs (E.T. alleluia).

B

Cf. Ps 89:14,17

At dawn, O Lord, fill us with your merciful love,
and we shall exult and rejoice all our days.
Let the favour of the Lord our God be upon us
and upon the work of our hands (E.T. alleluia).

C

Cf. Ps 144:2,9

I will bless you day after day, O Lord,
and praise your name for ever and ever,
for you are kind to all
and compassionate to all your creatures (E.T. alleluia).

Sign of the Cross

When the Entrance Antiphon is concluded, the Priest and the faithful, standing, sign themselves with the Sign of the Cross.

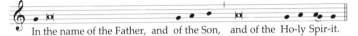

In the name of the Father, and of the Son, and of the Ho-ly Spir-it.

Priest: In the name of the Father, ✠ and of the Son, and of the Holy Spirit.

The people reply:

A-men.

Response: **Amen.**

Greeting

The Priest greets the people, saying:

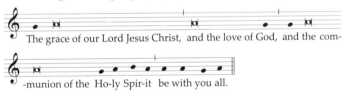

The grace of our Lord Jesus Christ, and the love of God, and the com-

-munion of the Ho-ly Spir-it be with you all.

Pr. The grace of our Lord Jesus Christ,
and the love of God,
and the communion of the Holy Spirit
be with you all.

Or:

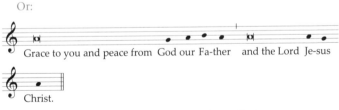

Grace to you and peace from God our Fa-ther and the Lord Je-sus

Christ.

Pr. Grace to you and peace from God our Father
and the Lord Jesus Christ.

Or:

The Lord be with you.

Pr. The Lord be with you.

The people reply:

And with your spir-it.

R. And with your spirit.

Then, in these or similar words, the Priest addresses the couple and those present to dispose them inwardly for the celebration of Marriage:

We have come rejoicing into the house of the Lord
for this celebration, dear brothers and sisters,
and now we stand with N. and N.
on the day they intend to form a home of their own.
For them this is a moment of unique importance.
So let us support them
with our affection,
with our friendship,
and with our prayer as their brothers and sisters.
Let us listen attentively with them
to the word that God speaks to us today.
Then, with holy Church,
let us humbly pray to God the Father,
through Christ our Lord,
for this couple, his servants,
that he lovingly accept them,
bless them,
and make them always one.

Or:

N. and N., the Church shares your joy
and warmly welcomes you,
together with your families and friends,
as today,

in the presence of God our Father,
you establish between yourselves
a lifelong partnership.
May the Lord hear you on this your joyful day.
May he send you help from heaven and protect you.
May he grant you your hearts' desire
and fulfil every one of your prayers.

The Penitential Act is omitted. The Gloria in excelsis (Glory to God in the highest) is said. If the marriage takes place without a Eucharist then the Gloria is omitted and the marriage continues with the Collect (pages 8-9).

The Gloria

Everyone sings, or recites together, this ancient Christian hymn:

Glo-ry to God in the high-est,

and on earth peace to peo-ple of good will.

We praise you,   we bless you,   we a-dore you,   we glo-ri-fy you,

we give you thanks for your great glo-ry,

Lord God, heav-en-ly King,   O God,   al-might-y Fa-ther.

Lord Je-sus Christ, On-ly Be-got-ten Son,

Lord God, Lamb of God,   Son of the Fa-ther,

you take a-way the sins of the world,   have mer-cy on us;

you take a-way the sins of the world,   re-ceive our prayer;

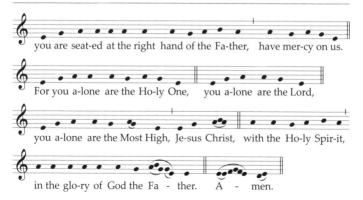

you are seat-ed at the right hand of the Fa-ther, have mer-cy on us.

For you a-lone are the Ho-ly One, you a-lone are the Lord,

you a-lone are the Most High, Je-sus Christ, with the Ho-ly Spir-it,

in the glo-ry of God the Fa - ther. A - men.

Glory to God in the highest,
and on earth peace to people of good will.

We praise you,
we bless you,
we adore you,
we glorify you,
we give you thanks for your great glory,
Lord God, heavenly King,
O God, almighty Father.

Lord Jesus Christ, Only Begotten Son,
Lord God, Lamb of God, Son of the Father,
you take away the sins of the world, have mercy on us;
you take away the sins of the world, receive our prayer;
you are seated at the right hand of the Father,
    have mercy on us.

For you alone are the Holy One,
you alone are the Lord,
you alone are the Most High,
Jesus Christ,
with the Holy Spirit,
in the glory of God the Father.
Amen.

The Collect

When this hymn is concluded, the Priest, says:

Pr. Let us pray.

    And all pray in silence with the Priest for a while.

    Then the Priest says one of the following Collect prayers, at the end of which the people acclaim:

R. Amen.

O God, who consecrated the bond of Marriage
by so great a mystery
that in the wedding covenant you foreshadow
the Sacrament of Christ and his Church,
grant, we pray, to these your servants,
that what they receive in faith they may live out in deeds.
Through Christ our Lord.†

    Or:

O God, who in creating the human race
willed that man and wife should be one,
join, we pray, in a bond of inseparable love
these your servants who are to be united in the
   covenant of Marriage,
so that, as you make their love fruitful,
they may become, by your grace, witnesses to charity itself.
Through Christ our Lord.

    Or:

Be attentive to our prayers, O Lord.
and in your kindness
pour out your grace on these your servants (N. and N.),
that, coming together before your altar,
they may be confirmed in love for one another.
Through Christ our Lord.

---

† This first Collect may not be used in the same celebration as the first
Nuptial Blessing (p.73).

Or:

Grant, we pray, almighty God,
that these your servants,
now to be joined by the Sacrament of Matrimony,
may grow in the faith they profess
and enrich your Church with faithful offspring.
Through Christ our Lord.

Or:

Be attentive to our prayers, O Lord,
and in your kindness uphold
what you have established for the increase
   of the human race,
so that the union you have created
may be kept safe by your assistance.
Through Christ our Lord.

Or:

O God, who since the beginning of the world
have blessed the increase of offspring,
show favour to our supplications
and pour forth the help of your blessing
on these your servants (N. and N.),
so that in the union of Marriage
they may be bound together
in mutual affection,
in likeness of mind,
and in shared holiness.
Through Christ our Lord.

The Liturgy of the Word

ALL SIT. Now one or two readings from Scripture are proclaimed, followed by a passage from the Gospel, in the normal fashion of the Liturgy of the Word, with this reservation: at least one of the readings chosen must refer explicitly to marriage. These readings are designated by an asterisk (*). The First Reading is normally from the Old Testament, but during Eastertide may be taken from the Book of Revelation. A Responsorial Psalm follows and then, if desired, a Second Reading from the New Testament. The Liturgy of the Word always concludes with a reading from the Gospel.

First Readings

1. Genesis 1:26-28,31a*

Male and female he created them.

God said, 'Let us make man in our own image, in the likeness of ourselves, and let them be masters of the fish of the sea, the birds of heaven, the cattle, all the wild beasts and all the reptiles that crawl upon the earth.'

God created man in the image of himself,
in the image of God he created him,
male and female he created them.

God blessed them, saying to them, 'Be fruitful, multiply, fill the earth and conquer it. Be masters of the fish of the sea, the birds of heaven and all living animals on the earth.' God saw all he had made, and indeed it was very good.

The word of the Lord.

R. **Thanks be to God.**

2. Genesis 2:18-24*

They become one body.

The Lord God said, 'It is not good that the man should be alone. I will make him a helpmate.' So from the soil the Lord God fashioned all the wild beasts and all the birds of heaven. These he brought to the man to see what he would call them; each one was to bear the name the man would give it. The man gave names to all the cattle, all the birds of heaven and all the wild beasts. But no helpmate suitable for man was found for him. So the Lord God made the man fall into a deep sleep. And while he slept, he took one of his ribs and enclosed it in flesh. The Lord God built the rib he had taken from the man into a woman, and brought her to the man. The man exclaimed:

'This at last is bone from my bones
and flesh from my flesh!
This is to be called woman,
for this was taken from man.'

This is why a man leaves his father and mother and joins himself to his wife, and they become one body.

The word of the Lord.

R. **Thanks be to God.**

3. Genesis 24:48-51,58-67*

Isaac loved Rebekah, and so he was consoled for the loss of his mother.

Abraham's servant said to Laban, 'I blessed the Lord, God of my master Abraham, who had so graciously led me to choose the daughter of my master's brother for his son. Now tell me whether you are prepared to show kindness and goodness to my master; if not, say so, and I shall know what to do.'

Laban and Bethuel replied, 'This is from the Lord; it is not in our power to say yes or no to you. Rebekah is there before you. Take her and go; and let her become the wife of your master's son, as the Lord has decreed'. They called Rebekah and asked her, 'Do you want to leave with this man?' 'I do,' she replied. Accordingly they let their sister Rebekah go, with her nurse, and Abraham's servant and his men. They blessed Rebekah in these words:

'Sister of ours, increase
to thousands and tens of thousands!
May your descendants gain possession
of the gates of their enemies!'

Rebekah and her servants stood up, mounted the camels, and followed the man. The servant took Rebekah and departed.

Isaac, who lived in the Negeb, had meanwhile come into the wilderness of the well of Lahai Roi. Now Isaac went walking in the fields as evening fell, and looking up saw camels approaching. And Rebekah looked up and saw Isaac. She jumped down from her camel, and asked the servant, 'Who is that man walking through the fields to meet us?' The servant replied, 'That is my master'; then she took her veil and hid her face. The servant told Isaac the whole story, and Isaac led Rebekah into his tent and made her his wife; and he loved her. And so Isaac was consoled for the loss of his mother.

The word of the Lord.

R. **Thanks be to God.**

4. **Tobit 7:6-14** *

The Lord of heaven favour you, my child, and grant you his grace and peace.

Raguel kissed Tobias and wept. Then finding words, he said, 'Blessings on you, child! You are the son of a noble father. How sad it is that someone so virtuous and full of good deeds should have gone blind!' He fell on the neck of his kinsman Tobias and wept. And his wife Edna wept for him, and so did his daughter Sarah. Raguel killed a sheep from the flock, and they gave Tobias and Raphael a warm-hearted welcome.

They washed and bathed and sat down to table. Then Tobias said to Raphael, 'Brother Azarias, will you ask Raguel to give me my sister Sarah?' Raguel overheard the words, and said to the young man, 'Eat and drink, and make the most of your evening; no one else has the right to take my daughter Sarah – no one but you, my brother. In any case I, for my own part, am not at liberty to give her to anyone else, since you are her next of kin. However, my boy, I must be frank with you: I have tried to find a husband for her seven times among our kinsmen, and all of them have died the first evening, on going to her room. But for the present, my boy, eat and drink; the Lord will grant you his grace and peace.' Tobias spoke out, 'I will not hear of eating and drinking till you have come to a decision about me.' Raguel answered, 'Very well. Since, as prescribed by the Book of Moses, she is given to you, heaven itself decrees she shall be yours. I shall therefore entrust your sister to you. From now you are her brother and she is your sister. She is given to you from today for ever. The Lord of heaven favour you tonight, my child, and grant you his grace and peace.' Raguel called for his daughter Sarah, took her by the hand and gave her to Tobias with these words, 'I entrust her to you; the law and the ruling recorded in the Book of Moses assign her to you as your wife. Take her; take her home to your father's house with a good conscience. The God of heaven grant you a good journey in peace.' Then he turned to her mother and asked her to fetch him writing paper. He drew up the marriage contract, how he gave his daughter as bride to Tobias according to the ordinance in the Law of Moses.

After this they began to eat and drink.

The word of the Lord.

R. **Thanks be to God.**

5. **Tobit 8:4b-8***

Bring us to old age together.

On the evening of their marriage, Tobias said to Sarah, 'You and I must pray and petition our Lord to win his grace and his protection.' They began praying for protection, and this was how he began:

> 'You are blessed, O God of our fathers;
> blessed, too, is your name
> for ever and ever.
> Let the heavens bless you
> and all things you have made
> for evermore.
> It was you who created Adam,
> you who created Eve his wife
> to be his help and support;
> and from these two the human race was born.
> It was you who said,
> "It is not good that the man should be alone;
> let us make him a helpmate like himself."
> And so I do not take my sister
> for any lustful motive;
> I do it in singleness of heart.
> Be kind enough to have pity on her and on me
> and bring us to old age together.'

And together they said, 'Amen, Amen'.

> The word of the Lord.

R. **Thanks be to God.**

6. **Proverbs 31:10-13,19-20,30-31***

The woman who fears the Lord is the one to praise.

> A perfect wife – who can find her?
> She is far beyond the price of pearls.
> Her husband's heart has confidence in her,
> from her he will derive no little profit.
> Advantage and not hurt she brings him
> all the days of her life.

She is always busy with wool and with flax,
she does her work with eager hands.
She sets her hands to the distaff,
her fingers grasp the spindle.
She holds out her hands to the poor,
she opens her arms to the needy.
Charm is deceitful, and beauty empty;
the woman who is wise is the one to praise.
Give her a share in what her hands have worked for,
and let her works tell her praises at the city gates.

The word of the Lord.

R. **Thanks be to God.**

7. **Song of Songs 2:8-10,14,16a; 8:6-7a**

Love is strong as death.

I hear my Beloved.
See how he comes
leaping on the mountains,
bounding over the hills.
My Beloved is like a gazelle,
like a young stag.
See where he stands
behind our wall.
He looks in at the window,
he peers through the lattice.
My Beloved lifts up his voice,
he says to me,
'Come then, my love,
my lovely one, come.'
My dove, hiding in the clefts of the rock,
in the coverts of the cliff,
show me your face,
let me hear your voice;
for your voice is sweet
and your face is beautiful.'

My Beloved is mine and I am his.

Set me like a seal on your heart,
like a seal on your arm.
For love is strong as Death,
jealousy relentless as Sheol.
The flash of it is a flash of fire,
a flame of the Lord himself.
Love no flood can quench,
no torrents drown.

The word of the Lord.

R. **Thanks be to God.**

8. Ecclesiasticus [Sirach] 26:1-4,16-21 *

Like the sun rising is the beauty of a good wife in her well-kept house.

Happy the husband of a really good wife;
the number of his days will be doubled.
A perfect wife is the joy of her husband,
he will live out the years of his life in peace.
A good wife is the best of portions,
reserved for those who fear the Lord;
rich or poor, they will be glad of heart,
cheerful of face, whatever the season.
The grace of a wife will charm her husband,
her accomplishments will make him the stronger.
A silent wife is a gift from the Lord,
no price can be put on a well-trained character.
A modest wife is a boon twice over,
a chaste character cannot be weighed on scales.
Like the sun rising over the mountains of the Lord
is the beauty of a good wife in a well-kept house.

The word of the Lord.

R. **Thanks be to God.**

9. Jeremiah 31:31-32a,33-34a

I will make a new covenant with the House of Israel and the House of Judah.

See, the days are coming – it is the Lord who speaks – when I will make a new covenant with the House of Israel and the House of Judah, but not a covenant like the one I made with their ancestors on the day I took them by the hand to bring them out of the land of Egypt. No, this is the covenant I will make with the House of Israel when those days arrive – it is the Lord who speaks. Deep within them I will plant my Law, writing it on their hearts. Then I will be their God and they shall be my people. There will be no further need for neighbour to try to teach neighbour, or brother to say to brother, 'Learn to know the Lord!' No, they will all know me, the least no less than the greatest – it is the Lord who speaks.

The word of the Lord.

R. **Thanks be to God.**

It is appropriate to use this reading in the Easter Season.

10. Apocalypse [Revelation] 19:1,5-9a

Happy are those who invited to the wedding feast of the Lamb.

I, John, seemed to hear the great sound of a huge crowd in heaven, singing, 'Alleluia! Victory and glory and power to our God!'

Then a voice came from the throne; it said, 'Praise our God, you servants of his and all who, great or small, revere him.' And I seemed to hear the voices of a huge crowd, like the sound of the ocean or the great roar of thunder, answering, 'Alleluia! The reign of the Lord our God Almighty has begun; let us be glad and joyful and give praise to God, because this is the time for the marriage of the Lamb. His bride is ready, and she has been able to dress herself in dazzling white linen, because her linen is made of the good deeds of the saints.' The angel said, 'Write this: Happy are those who are invited to the wedding feast of the Lamb.'

The word of the Lord.

R. **Thanks be to God.**

Second Readings

1. Romans 8:31b-35,37-39a

Nothing can come between us and the love of Christ?

With God on our side who can be against us? Since God did not spare his own Son, but gave him up to benefit us all, we may be certain, after such a gift, that he will not refuse anything he can give. Could anyone accuse those that God has chosen? When God acquits, could anyone condemn? Could Christ Jesus? No! He not only died for us – he rose from the dead, and there at God's right hand he stands and pleads for us.

Nothing therefore can come between us and the love of Christ, even if we are troubled or worried, or being persecuted, or lacking food or clothes, or being threatened or even attacked. These are the trials through which we triumph, by the power of him who loved us.

For I am certain of this: neither death nor life, no angel, no prince, nothing that exists, nothing still to come, not any power, or height or depth, nor any created thing, can ever come between us and the love of God made visible in Christ Jesus our Lord.

The word of the Lord.

R. **Thanks be to God.**

2. Romans 12:1-2,9-18 or 12:1-2,9-13

Offering your living bodies as a holy sacrifice, truly pleasing to him.

Think of God's mercy, my brothers, and worship him, I beg you, in a way that is worthy of thinking beings, by offering your living bodies as a holy sacrifice, truly pleasing to God. Do not model yourselves on the behaviour of the world around you, but let your behaviour change, modelled by your new mind. This is the only way to discover the will of God and know what is good, what it is that God wants, what is the perfect thing to do.

Do not let your love be a pretence, but sincerely prefer good to evil. Love each other as much as brothers should, and have a profound respect for each other. Work for the Lord with untiring effort and with great earnestness of spirit. If you have hope, this will make you cheerful. Do not give up if trials come; and keep on praying. If any of the saints are in need you must share with them; and you should make hospitality your special care.*

Bless those who persecute you: never curse them, bless them. Rejoice with those who rejoice and be sad with those in sorrow. Treat everyone with equal kindness; never be condescending but make real friends with the poor. Do not allow yourself to become self-satisfied. Never repay evil with evil but let everyone see that you are interested only in the highest ideals. Do all you can to live at peace with everyone.

The word of the Lord.

R. **Thanks be to God.**

*The shorter form of this reading ends here.

3. **Romans 15:1b-3a, 5-7, 13**

Treat each other as Christ.

We should not think of ourselves. Each of us should think of his neighbours and help them to become stronger Christians. Christ did not think of himself. And may he who helps us when we refuse to give up, help you all to be tolerant with each other, following the example of Christ Jesus, so that united in mind and voice you may give glory to the God and Father of our Lord Jesus Christ.

It can only be to God's glory, then, for you to treat each other in the same friendly way as Christ treated you.

May the God of hope bring you such joy and peace in your faith that the power of the Holy Spirit will remove all bounds to hope.

The word of the Lord.

R. **Thanks be to God.**

4. 1 Corinthians 6:13c-15a,17-20

Your body is the temple of the Holy Spirit.

The body is not meant for fornication; it is for the Lord, and the Lord for the body. God, who raised the Lord from the dead, will by his power raise us up too.

You know, surely, that your bodies are members making up the body of Christ. But anyone who is joined to the Lord is one spirit with him.

Keep away from fornication. All the other sins are committed outside the body; but to fornicate is to sin against your own body. Your body, you know, is the temple of the Holy Spirit, who is in you since you received him from God. You are not your own property; you have been bought and paid for. That is why you should use your body for the glory of God.

The word of the Lord.

R. **Thanks be to God.**

5. 1 Corinthians 12:31-13:8a

If I am without love, it will do me no good whatever.

Be ambitious for the higher gifts. And I am going to show you a way that is better than any of them.

If I have all the eloquence of men or of angels, but speak without love, I am simply a gong booming or a cymbal clashing. If I have the gift of prophecy, understanding all the mysteries there are, and knowing everything, and if I have faith in all its fullness, to move mountains, but without love, then I am nothing at all. If I give away all that I possess, piece by piece, and if I even let them take my body to burn it, but am without love, it will do me no good whatever.

Love is always patient and kind; it is never jealous; love is never boastful or conceited; it is never rude or selfish; it does not take offence, and is not resentful. Love takes no pleasure in other people's sins but delights in the truth; it is always ready to excuse, to trust, to hope, and to endure whatever comes.

Love does not come to an end.

The word of the Lord.

R. **Thanks be to God.**

6. Ephesians 4:1-6

One Body, one Lord, one faith, one baptism.

I, the prisoner in the Lord, implore you to lead a life worthy of your vocation. Bear with one another charitably, in complete selflessness, gentleness and patience. Do all you can to preserve the unity of the Spirit by the peace that binds you together. There is one Body, one Spirit, just as you were all called into one and the same hope when you were called. There is one Lord, one faith, one baptism, and one God who is Father of all, through all and within all.

The word of the Lord.

R. **Thanks be to God**.

7. Ephesians 5:2a,21-33* or 5:2a,25-32*

This mystery has many implications and I am saying it applies to Christ and the Church.

Follow Christ by loving as he loved you, giving himself up in our place.* Give way to one another in obedience to Christ. Wives should regard their husbands as they regard the Lord, since as Christ is head of the Church and saves the whole body, so is a husband the head of his wife; and as the Church submits to Christ, so should wives to their husbands, in everything.* Husbands should love their wives just as Christ loved the Church and sacrificed himself for her to make her holy. He made her clean by washing her in water with a form of words, so that when he took her to himself she would be glorious, with no speck or wrinkle or anything like that, but holy and faultless. In the same way, husbands must love their wives as they love their own bodies; for a man to love his wife is for him to love himself. A man never hates his own body, but he feeds it and looks after it; and that is the way Christ treats the Church, because it is his body – and we are its living parts. For this reason, a man must leave his father and mother and be joined to his wife, and the two will become one body. This mystery has many implications; but I am saying it applies to Christ and the Church.† To sum up; you too, each one of you, must love his wife as he loves himself; and let every wife respect her husband.

The word of the Lord.

R. **Thanks be to God.**

*†The verses between the asterisks and after the dagger may be omitted.

8. **Philippians 4:4-9**

The God of peace will be with you.

I want you to be happy, always happy in the Lord; I repeat, what I want is your happiness. Let your tolerance be evident to everyone: the Lord is very near. There is no need to worry; but if there is anything you need, pray for it, asking God for it with prayer and thanksgiving, and that peace of God, which is so much greater than we can understand, will guard your hearts and your thoughts, in Christ Jesus.

Finally, brothers, fill your minds with everything that is true, everything that is noble, everything that is good and pure, everything that we love and honour, and everything that can be thought virtuous or worthy of praise. Keep doing all the things that you learnt from me and have been taught by me and have heard or seen that I do. Then the God of peace will be with you.

The word of the Lord.

R. **Thanks be to God.**

9. **Colossians 3:12-17**

Over all these, to keep them together and complete them, put on love.

You are God's chosen race, his saints; he loves you, and you should be clothed in sincere compassion, in kindness and humility, gentleness and patience. Bear with one another; forgive each other as soon as a quarrel begins. The Lord has forgiven you; now you must do the same. Over all these clothes, to keep them together and complete them, put on love. And may the peace of Christ reign in your hearts, because it is for this that you were called together as parts of one body. Always be thankful.

Let the message of Christ, in all its richness, find a home with you. Teach each other, and advise each other, in all wisdom. With gratitude in your hearts sing psalms and hymns and inspired songs to God; and never say or do anything except in the name of the Lord Jesus, giving thanks to God the Father through him.

The word of the Lord.

R. **Thanks be to God.**

10. **Hebrews 13:1-4a, 5-6b**

Marriage is to be honoured by all.

Continue to love each other like brothers, and remember always to welcome strangers, for by doing this, some people have entertained angels without knowing it. Keep in mind those who are in prison, as though you were in prison with them; and those who are being badly treated, since you too are in the one body. Marriage is to be honoured by all, and marriages are to be kept undefiled.

Put greed out of your lives and be content with whatever you have; God himself has said: I will not fail you or desert you, and so we can say with confidence: With the Lord to help me, I fear nothing.

The word of the Lord.

R. **Thanks be to God.**

11. **1 Peter 3:1-9** *

You should all agree among yourselves and be sympathetic; love the brothers.

Wives should be obedient to their husbands. Then, if there are some husbands who have not yet obeyed the word, they may find themselves won over, without a word spoken, by the way their wives behave, when they see how faithful and conscientious they are. Do not dress up for show: doing up your hair, wearing gold bracelets and fine clothes; all this should be inside, in a person's heart, imperishable: the ornament of a sweet and gentle disposition — this is what is precious in the sight of God. That was how the holy women of the past dressed themselves attractively — they hoped in God and were tender and obedient to their husbands; like Sarah, who was obedient to Abraham, and called him her lord. You are now her children, as long as you live good lives and do not give way to fear or worry.

In the same way, husbands must always treat their wives with consideration in their life together, respecting a woman as one who, though she may be the weaker partner, is equally an heir to the life of grace. This will stop anything from coming in the way of your prayers.

Finally: you should all agree among yourselves and be sympathetic; love the brothers, have compassion and be self-effacing. Never pay back one wrong with another one; instead, pay back with a blessing. That is what you are called to do, so that you inherit a blessing yourself.

The word of the Lord.

R. **Thanks be to God.**

12. **1 John 3:18-24**

Our love is to be something real and active.

My children,
our love is not to be just words or mere talk,
but something real and active;
only by this can we be certain
that we are the children of the truth
and be able to quieten our conscience in his presence,
whatever accusations it may raise against us,
because God is greater than our conscience
    and he knows everything.
My dear people,
if we cannot be condemned by our own conscience,
we need not be afraid in God's presence,
and whatever we ask him,
we shall receive,

because we keep his commandments
and live the kind of life that he wants.
His commandments are these:
that we believe in the name of his Son Jesus Christ
and that we love one another
as he told us to.
Whoever keeps his commandments
lives in God and God lives in him.
We know that he lives in us
by the Spirit that he has given us.

The word of the Lord.

R. **Thanks be to God.**

13. **1 John 4:7-12**

God is love.

My dear people,
let us love one another
since love comes from God
and everyone who loves is begotten by God and knows God.
Anyone who fails to love can never have known God,
because God is love.
God's love for us was revealed
when God sent into the world his only Son
so that we could have life through him;
this is the love I mean:
not our love for God,
but God's love for us when he sent his Son
to be the sacrifice that takes our sins away.
My dear people,
since God has loved us so much,
we too should love one another.
No one has ever seen God;
but as long as we love one another
God will live in us
and his love will be complete in us.

The word of the Lord.

R. **Thanks be to God.**

Responsorial Psalms

After the first reading, one of the following is sung or said:

1. **Psalm 32(33):12,18,20-21,22. R. v.5b**

Response: **The Lord fills the earth with his love.**

They are happy, whose God is the Lord,
the people he has chosen as his own.
The Lord looks on those who revere him,
on those who hope in his love. (R.)

Our soul is waiting for the Lord.
The Lord is our help and our shield.
In him do our hearts find joy.
We trust in his holy name. (R.)

May your love be upon us, O Lord,
as we place all our hope in you. (R.)

2. **Psalm 33(34):2-3,4-5,6-7,8-9. R. v.2a, alt. R. v.9a**

Response: **I will bless the Lord at all times.**

Or: **Taste and see that the Lord is good.**

I will bless the Lord at all times,
his praise always on my lips;
in the Lord my soul shall make its boast.
The humble shall hear and be glad. (R.)

Glorify the Lord with me.
Together let us praise his name.
I sought the Lord and he answered me;
from all my terrors he set me free. (R.)

Look towards him and be radiant;
let your faces not be abashed.
This poor man called; the Lord heard him
and rescued him from all his distress. (R.)

The angel of the Lord is encamped
around those who revere him, to rescue them.
Taste and see that the Lord is good.
He is happy who seeks refuge in him. (R.)

3. Psalm 102(103):1-2,8,13,17-18a. R. v.8a, alt. R. cf v.17

Response: **The Lord is compassion and love.**

Or: **The love of the Lord is everlasting
upon those who hold him in fear.**

My soul, give thanks to the Lord,
all my being, bless his holy name.
My soul, give thanks to the Lord
and never forget all his blessings. (R.)

The Lord is compassion and love,
slow to anger and rich in mercy.
As a father has compassion on his sons,
the Lord has pity on those who fear him. (R.)

The love of the Lord is everlasting
upon those who hold him in fear;
his justice reaches out to children's children
when they keep his covenant in truth. (R.)

4. Psalm 111(112):1-2,3-4,5-7a,7bc-8,9. R. cf v.1

Response: **Happy the man who takes delight
in the Lord's commands.**

Or (outside Lent): **Alleluia!**

Happy the man who fears the Lord,
who takes delight in his commands.
His sons will be powerful on earth;
the children of the upright are blessed. (R.)

Riches and wealth are in his house;
his justice stands firm for ever.
He is a light in the darkness for the upright:
he is generous, merciful and just. (R.)

The love of the Lord is everlasting,
he conducts his affairs with honour.
The just man will never waver:
he will be remembered for ever. (R.)

He has no fear of evil news;
with a firm heart he trusts in the Lord.
With a steadfast heart he will not fear;
he will see the downfall of his foes. (R.)

Open-handed, he gives to the poor;
his justice stands firm for ever.
His head will be raised in glory. (R.)

Response: **Happy the man who takes delight
in the Lord's commands.**

Or (outside Lent): **Alleluia!**

5. **Psalm 127(128):1-2,3,4-5ac,6a. R. cf v.1, alt. R. v.4**[*]

Response: **O blessed are those who fear the Lord!**

Or: **Indeed thus shall be blessed
the man who fears the Lord.**

O blessed are those who fear the Lord
and walk in his ways!
By the labour of your hands you shall eat.
You will be happy and prosper. (R.)

Your wife will be like a fruitful vine
in the heart of your house;
your children like shoots of the olive,
around your table. (R.)

Indeed thus shall be blessed
the man who fears the Lord.
May the Lord bless you from Zion
all the days of your life!
May you see your children's children. (R.)

6. **Psalm 144(145):8-9,10,15,17-18. R. v.9a**

Response: **How good is the Lord to all.**

The Lord is kind and full of compassion,
slow to anger, abounding in love.
How good is the Lord to all,
compassionate to all his creatures. (R.)

All your creatures shall thank you, O Lord,
and your friends shall repeat their blessing.
The eyes of all creatures look to you
and you give them their food in due time. (R.)

The Lord is just in all his ways
and loving in all his deeds.
He is close to all who call him,
who call on him from their hearts. (R.)

7. **Psalm 148:1-2,3-4,9-10,11-13ab,13c-14a. R. v.13a**

Response: **Let them praise the name of the Lord.**
Or (outside Lent): **Alleluia!**

Praise the Lord from the heavens,
praise him in the heights.
Praise him, all his angels,
praise him, all his host. (R.)

Praise him, sun and moon,
praise him, shining stars.
Praise him, highest heavens
and the waters above the heavens. (R.)

All mountains and hills,
all fruit trees and cedars,
beasts, wild and tame,
reptiles and birds on the wing. (R.)

All earth's kings and peoples,
earth's princes and rulers;
young men and maidens,
old men together with children. (R.)

Let them praise the name of the Lord
for he alone is exalted.
The splendour of his name
reaches beyond heaven and earth. (R.)

Acclamations before the Gospel

ALL STAND. The congregation proclaims that is ready to hear the gospel message in one of the following forms. Wherever possible, this acclamation should be sung.

Outside the season of Lent

1. **Alleluia, alleluia!**
   Everyone who loves
   is begotten by God,
   and knows God.
   Alleluia! (1 Jn 4:7b)

2. **Alleluia, alleluia!**
   As long as we love
     one another
   God will live in us,
   and his love will be
     complete in us.
   Alleluia! (1 Jn 4:12)

3. **Alleluia, alleluia!**
   Anyone who lives in love,
   lives in God,
   and God lives in him.
   Alleluia! (1 Jn 4:16)

4. **Alleluia, alleluia!**
   God is love;
   let us love one another
   as God has loved us.
   Alleluia! (1 Jn 4:8b,11)

During the season of Lent

1. **Praise to you, O Christ,
   king of eternal glory.**
   Everyone who loves
   is begotten by God,
   and knows God.
   Praise to you, O Christ...
   (1 Jn 4:7b)

2. **Praise to you, O Christ,
   king of eternal glory.**
   As long as we love
     one another
   God will live in us,
   and his love will be
     complete in us.
   Praise to you, O Christ...
   (1 Jn 4:12)

3. **Praise to you, O Christ,
   king of eternal glory.**
   Anyone who lives in love,
   lives in God,
   and God lives in him.
   Praise to you, O Christ...
   (1 Jn 4:16)

4. **Praise to you, O Christ,
   king of eternal glory.**
   God is love;
   let us love one another
   as God has loved us.
   Praise to you, O Christ...
   (1 Jn 4:8,11)

Before reading the Gospel, the Deacon or Priest greets the people.

P. The Lord be with you.
R. And with your spirit.

He then announces the Gospel from which his reading is chosen. The people acclaim: **Glory to you, O Lord.**

Readings from the Gospels

1. Matthew 5:1-12a

Rejoice and be glad, for your reward will be great in heaven.

Seeing the crowds, Jesus went up the hill. There he sat down and was joined by his disciples. Then he began to speak. This is what he taught them:

'How happy are the poor in spirit;
theirs is the kingdom of heaven.
Happy the gentle:
they shall have the earth for their heritage.
Happy those who mourn:
they shall be comforted.
Happy those who hunger and thirst for what is right:
they shall be satisfied.
Happy the merciful:
they shall have mercy shown them.
Happy the pure in heart:
they shall see God.
Happy the peacemakers:
they shall be called sons of God.
Happy those who are persecuted in the cause of right:
theirs is the kingdom of heaven.

'Happy are you when people abuse you and persecute you and speak all kinds of calumny against you on my account. Rejoice and be glad, for your reward will be great in heaven.'

The Gospel of the Lord.

R. **Praise to you, Lord Jesus Christ.**

2. Matthew 5:13-16

You are the light of the world.

Jesus said to his disciples: 'You are the salt of the earth. But if salt becomes tasteless, what can make it salty again? It is good for nothing, and can only be thrown out to be trampled underfoot by men.

'You are the light of the world. A city built on a hilltop cannot be hidden. No one lights a lamp to put it under a tub;

they put it on the lamp-stand where it shines for everyone in the house. In the same way your light must shine in the sight of men, so that, seeing your good works, they may give the praise to your Father in heaven.'

The Gospel of the Lord.

R. **Praise to you, Lord Jesus Christ.**

3. Matthew 7:21,24-29 or 7:21,24-25

He built his house on rock.

Jesus said to his disciples:

'It is not those who say to me, "Lord, Lord," who will enter the kingdom of heaven, but the person who does the will of my Father in heaven.

'Therefore, everyone who listens to these words of mine and acts on them will be like a sensible man who built his house on rock. Rain came down, floods rose, gales blew and hurled themselves against that house, and it did not fall: it was founded on rock.* But everyone who listens to these words of mine and does not act on them will be like a stupid man who built his house on sand. Rain came down, floods rose, gales blew and struck that house, and it fell; and what a fall it had!'

Jesus had now finished what he wanted to say, and his teaching made a deep impression on the people because he taught them with authority, and not like their own scribes.

The Gospel of the Lord.

R. **Praise to you, Lord Jesus Christ.**

*The shorter form ends here.

4. Matthew 19:3-6*

What God has united, man must not divide.

Some Pharisees approached Jesus, and to test him they said, 'Is it against the Law for a man to divorce his wife on any pretext whatever?' He answered, 'Have you not read that the creator from the beginning made them male and female and that he said: This is why a man must leave father and mother, and cling to his wife, and the two become one body? They are no longer two, therefore, but one body. So then, what God has united, man must not divide.'

The Gospel of the Lord.

R. **Praise to you, Lord Jesus Christ.**

5. Matthew 22:35-40

This is the greatest and the first commandment. The second resembles it.

A lawyer, to disconcert Jesus, put a question, 'Master, which is the greatest commandment of the Law?' Jesus said, 'You must love the Lord your God with all your heart, with all your soul, and with all your mind. This is the greatest and the first commandment. The second resembles it: You must love your neighbour as yourself. On these two commandments hang the whole Law, and the Prophets also.'

The Gospel of the Lord.

R. **Praise to you, Lord Jesus Christ.**

6. Mark 10:6-9*

They are no longer two, but one body.

Jesus said, 'From the beginning of creation God made them male and female. This is why a man must leave father and mother, and the two become one body. They are no longer two, therefore, but one body. So then, what God has united, man must not divide.'

The Gospel of the Lord.

R. **Praise to you, Lord Jesus Christ.**

7. John 2:1-11*

This was the first of the signs given by Jesus - at Cana in Galilee.

There was a wedding at Cana in Galilee. The mother of Jesus was there, and Jesus and his disciples had also been invited. When they ran out of wine, since the wine provided for the wedding was all finished, the mother of Jesus said to him, 'They have no wine.' Jesus said, 'Woman why turn to me?

My hour has not come yet.' His mother said to the servants, 'Do whatever he tells you.' There were six stone water jars standing there, meant for the ablutions that are customary among the Jews; each could hold twenty or thirty gallons. Jesus said to the servants, 'Fill the jars with water,' and they filled them to the brim. 'Draw some out now' he told them, 'and take it to the steward.' They did this; the steward tasted the water, and it had turned into wine. Having no idea where it came from – only the servants who had drawn the water knew – the steward called the bridegroom and said, 'People generally serve the best wine first, and keep the cheaper sort till the guests have had plenty to drink; but you have kept the best wine till now.'

This was the first of the signs given by Jesus: it was given at Cana in Galilee. He let his glory be seen, and his disciples believed in him.

The Gospel of the Lord.

R. **Praise to you, Lord Jesus Christ.**

8. **John 15:9-12**

Remain in my love.

Jesus said to his disciples:

'As the Father has loved me,
so I have loved you.
Remain in my love.
If you keep my commandments
you will remain in my love,
just as I have kept my Father's commandments
and remain in his love.
I have told you this
so that my own joy may be in you
and your joy be complete.
This is my commandment:
love one another,
as I have loved you.'

The Gospel of the Lord.

R. **Praise to you, Lord Jesus Christ.**

9. **John 15:12-16**

What I command you is to love one another.

Jesus said to his disciples:

'This is my commandment:
love one another,
as I have loved you.
A man can have no greater love
than to lay down his life for his friends.
You are my friends,
if you do what I command you.
I shall not call you servants any more,
because a servant does not know
his master's business;
I call you friends,
because I have made known to you
everything I have learnt from my Father.
You did not choose me,
no, I chose you;
and I commissioned you
to go out and to bear fruit,
fruit that will last;
and then the Father will give you
anything you ask him in my name.'

The Gospel of the Lord.

R. **Praise to you, Lord Jesus Christ**.

10. **John 17:20-26 or 17:20-23**

May they be completely one.

Jesus raised his eyes to heaven and said:
'Holy Father,
I pray not only for these,
but for those also
who through their words will believe in me.
May they all be one.
Father, may they be one in us
as you are in me and I am in you,

so that the world may believe it was you who sent me.
I have given them the glory you gave to me,
that they may be one as we are one.
With me in them and you in me,
may they be so completely one
that the world will realise that it was you who sent me
and that I have loved them as much as you loved me.*
Father,
I want those you have given me
to be with me where I am,
so that they may always see the glory
you have given me
because you loved me
before the foundation of the world.
Father, Righteous One,
the world has not known you,
but I have known you,
and these have known
that you have sent me.
I have made your name known to them
and will continue to make it known,
so that the love with which you loved me may be in them,
and so that I may be in them.'

The Gospel of the Lord.

R. Praise to you, Lord Jesus Christ.

*The shorter form ends here.

Homily

THE PEOPLE NOW SIT.

The Priest gives a Homily drawn from the sacred texts. He speaks about the mystery of Christian marriage, the dignity of married love, the grace of the sacrament and the responsibilities of married people, keeping in mind the circumstances of this particular marriage.

The Celebration of Marriage

Address

With ALL STANDING, including the couple and the witnesses, who are positioned near them, the Priest addresses the couple in these or similar words:

Dearly beloved,
you have come together into the house of the Church,
so that in the presence of the Church's minister
    and the community
your intention to enter into Marriage
may be strengthened by the Lord with a sacred seal.
Christ abundantly blesses the love that binds you.
Through a special Sacrament,
he enriches and strengthens
those he has already consecrated by Holy Baptism,
that they may be faithful to each other for ever
and assume all the responsibilities of married life.
And so, in the presence of the Church,
I ask you to state your intentions.

The Questions before the Consent

The Priest then questions them about their freedom of choice, fidelity to each other, and the acceptance and upbringing of children, and each responds separately.

N. and N., have you come here to enter into Marriage
without coercion,
freely and wholeheartedly?

The bridegroom and bride each say:

I have.

Addressing the bridegroom, the Priest says:

N., are you resolved to take N. to be your wife:
to love her, comfort her, honour and protect her,
and forsaking all others, to be faithful to her
as long as you both shall live?

The bridegroom replies:

I am.

Next the Priest, asks the bride:

N., are you resolved to take N. to be your husband:
to love him, comfort him, honour and protect him,
and forsaking all others, to be faithful to him
as long as you both shall live?

The bride replies:

I am.

The following question may be omitted, if circumstances
suggest this, for example if the couple are advanced in years.

Are you prepared to accept children lovingly from God
and to bring them up
according to the law of Christ and his Church?

The bridegroom and bride each say:

I am.

The Civil Declaration of Freedom

The law of England and Wales requires the couple to make a declaration of their freedom to marry, in one of the following forms. Names and surnames must be used.

Form A

First, the Priest asks the bridegroom:

Are you, A.B., free lawfully to marry C.D.?

The bridegroom replies:

I am.

Next, the Priest asks the bride:

Are you, C.D., free lawfully to marry A.B.?

The bride replies:

I am.

Or:

Form B

The bridegroom reads the following or repeats the words after the Priest:

I do solemnly declare
that I know not of any lawful impediment why I, A.B.,
may not be joined in matrimony to C.D.

The bride reads the following or repeats the words after the Priest:

I do solemnly declare
that I know not of any lawful impediment why I, C.D.,
may not be joined in matrimony to A.B.

Or:

Form C

The bridegroom says:

I declare that I know of no legal reason why I, A.B., may not be joined in marriage to C.D.

The bride says:

I declare that I know of no legal reason why I, C.D., may not be joined in marriage to A.B.

Consent

The Priest invites them to declare their consent:

Since it is your intention to enter the covenant
of Holy Matrimony,
join your right hands and declare your consent
before God and his Church.

The couple face each other. The groom and bride read the following, or repeat the words after the Priest. Names and surnames must be used. They join their right hands.

Form A

The bridegroom says:

I call upon these persons here present to witness
that I, A.B., do take thee, C.D.,
to be my lawful wedded wife,
to have and to hold from this day forward
for better, for worse,
for richer, for poorer,
in sickness and in health,
to love and to cherish
till death do us part.

The bride says:

I call upon these persons here present to witness
that I, C.D., do take thee, A.B.,
to be my lawful wedded husband,
to have and to hold from this day forward,
for better, for worse,
for richer, for poorer,
in sickness and in health,
to love and to cherish
till death do us part.

Or:

Form B

The bridegroom says:

I, A.B., take you (thee), C.D., to be my wedded wife
to have and to hold from this day forward,
for better, for worse,
for richer, for poorer,
in sickness and in health,
to love and to cherish
till death do us part.

The bride says:

I, C.D., take you (thee), A.B., to be my wedded husband
to have and to hold from this day forward,
for better, for worse,
for richer, for poorer,
in sickness and in health,
to love and to cherish
till death do us part.

The Reception of the Consent

Then, receiving their consent, the Priest says to the bride
and bridegroom:

May the Lord in his kindness strengthen the consent
you have declared before the Church,
and graciously bring to fulfilment his blessing within you.
What God joins together, let no one put asunder.

Or:

May the God of Abraham, the God of Isaac,
    the God of Jacob,
the God who joined together our first parents in paradise,
strengthen and bless in Christ
the consent you have declared before the Church,
so that what God joins together,
    no one may put asunder.

The Priest invites those present to praise God:

Let us bless the Lord.

All reply:

Thanks be to God.

Another acclamation may be sung or said.

The Blessing and Giving of Rings

The Priest says:

May the Lord bless ✠ these rings,
which you will give to each other
as a sign of love and fidelity.
R. Amen.

Or:

Bless, O Lord, these rings,
which we bless ✠ in your name,
so that those who wear them
may remain entirely faithful to each other,
abide in peace and in your will,
and live always in mutual charity.
Through Christ our Lord.

Or:

Bless ✠ and sanctify your servants
in their love, O Lord,
and let these rings, a sign of their faithfulness,
remind them of their love for one another.
Through Christ our Lord.

He sprinkles the rings, as the circumstances so suggest,
and gives them to the bride and bridegroom.

The husband places his wife's ring on her ring finger,
saying, as the circumstances so suggest:

N., I give you this ring as a sign of our marriage:
with my body I honour you,
all that I am I give to you,
and all that I have I share with you,
in the name of the Father, and of the Son,
    and of the Holy Spirit.
R. Amen.

Likewise, the wife places her husband's ring on his ring finger, saying, as the circumstances so suggest:

N., I give you this ring as a sign of our marriage:
with my body I honour you,
all that I am I give to you,
and all that I have I share with you,
in the name of the Father, and of the Son,
   and of the Holy Spirit.
R. Amen.

Or:

The husband places his wife's ring on her ring finger, saying, as the circumstances so suggest:

N., receive this ring
as a sign of my love and fidelity.
In the name of the Father, and of the Son,
and of the Holy Spirit.

Likewise, the wife places her husband's ring on his ring finger, saying, as the circumstances so suggest:

N., receive this ring
as a sign of my love and fidelity.
In the name of the Father, and of the Son,
and of the Holy Spirit.

The Universal Prayer (Bidding Prayers)

Various intentions for prayer are introduced by the Deacon or other minister. Some examples are given below.

Priest:

Dear brothers and sisters,
as we call to mind the special gift of grace and charity
by which God has been pleased to crown and consecrate
the love of our sister N. and our brother N.,
let us commend them to the Lord.

The Deacon or other Minister continues:

That these faithful Christians, N. and N.,
newly joined in Holy Matrimony,
may always enjoy health and well-being,
let us pray to the Lord.

R. Lord, we ask you, hear our prayer.

Or another appropriate response of the people.

That he will bless their covenant
as he chose to sanctify marriage at Cana in Galilee,
let us pray to the Lord. R.

That they be granted perfect and fruitful love,
peace and strength,
and that they bear faithful witness
    to the name of Christian,
let us pray to the Lord. R.

That the Christian people
may grow in virtue day by day
and that all who are burdened by any need
may receive the help of grace from above,
let us pray to the Lord. R.

That the grace of the Sacrament
will be renewed by the Holy Spirit
in all married persons here present,
let us pray to the Lord. R.

Priest:

Graciously pour out upon this husband and wife, O Lord,
the Spirit of your love,
to make them one heart and one soul,
so that nothing whatever may divide those
you have joined and no harm come to those you have filled
with your blessing.
Through Christ our Lord.

R. Amen.

Or:

Priest:

Dear brothers and sisters,
let us accompany this new family with our prayers,
that the mutual love of this couple may grow daily
and that God in his kindness
will sustain all families throughout the world.

The Deacon or other Minister continues:

For this bride and groom,
and for their well-being as a family,
let us pray to the Lord.
R. Lord, we ask you, hear our prayer.

Or another appropriate response of the people.

For their relatives and friends,
and for all who have assisted this couple,
let us pray to the Lord. R.

For young people preparing to enter Marriage,
and for all whom the Lord is calling
    to another state in life,
let us pray to the Lord. R.

For all families throughout the world
and for lasting peace among all people,
let us pray to the Lord. R.

For all members of our families
who have passed from this world,
and for all the departed,
let us pray to the Lord. R.

For the Church, the holy People of God,
and for unity among all Christians,
let us pray to the Lord. R.

Priest:

Lord Jesus, who are present in our midst,
as N. and N. seal their union
accept our prayer
and fill us with your Spirit.
Who live and reign for ever and ever.
R. Amen.

If the marriage takes place without a Eucharist then it continues
with the **Nuptial Blessing**, p. 73.

The Creed

On Sundays and Solemnities the Profession of Faith is made after the Universal Prayer.

The Niceno-Constantinopolitan Creed

I believe in one God,
the Father almighty,
maker of heaven and earth,
of all things visible and invisible.

I believe in one Lord Jesus Christ,
the Only Begotten Son of God,
born of the Father before all ages.
God from God, Light from Light,
true God from true God,
begotten, not made, consubstantial with the Father;
through him all things were made.
For us men and for our salvation
he came down from heaven,

At the words that follow, up to and including and became man, all bow.

and by the Holy Spirit was incarnate of the Virgin Mary,
and became man.

For our sake he was crucified under Pontius Pilate,
he suffered death and was buried,
and rose again on the third day
in accordance with the Scriptures.
He ascended into heaven
and is seated at the right hand of the Father.
He will come again in glory
to judge the living and the dead
and his kingdom will have no end.

I believe in the Holy Spirit, the Lord, the giver of life,
who proceeds from the Father and the Son,
who with the Father and the Son is adored and glorified,
who has spoken through the prophets.

I believe in one, holy, catholic and apostolic Church.
I confess one Baptism for the forgiveness of sins
and I look forward to the resurrection of the dead
and the life of the world to come. Amen.

The Apostles' Creed

Instead of the Niceno-Constantinopolitan Creed, especially during
Lent and Easter Time, the Apostles' Creed may be used.

I believe in God,
the Father almighty
Creator of heaven and earth,
and in Jesus Christ, his only Son, our Lord,

At the words that follow, up to and including the Virgin Mary, all bow.

who was conceived by the Holy Spirit,
born of the Virgin Mary,
suffered under Pontius Pilate,
was crucified, died and was buried;
he descended into hell;
on the third day he rose again from the dead;
he ascended into heaven,
and is seated at the right hand of God the Father almighty;
from there he will come to judge the living and the dead.

I believe in the Holy Spirit,
the holy catholic Church,
the communion of saints,
the forgiveness of sins,
the resurrection of the body,
and life everlasting. Amen.

The Liturgy of the Eucharist

After the Prayer of the Faithful, THE PEOPLE SIT and the Offertory Chant begins. The faithful express their participation by making an offering, bringing forward bread and wine for the celebration of the Eucharist and perhaps other gifts to relieve the needs of the Church and the poor. These gifts may be presented to the Priest by the bride and bridegroom.

The Priest, standing at the altar, takes the paten with the bread and holds it slightly raised above the altar with both hands, saying in a low voice:

Pr. Blessed are you, Lord God of all creation,
for through your goodness we have received
the bread we offer you:
fruit of the earth and work of human hands,
it will become for us the bread of life.

If, however, the Offertory Chant is not sung, the Priest may speak these words aloud at the end, the people may acclaim:

R. **Blessed be God for ever.**

The Priest then takes the chalice and holds it slightly raised above the altar with both hands, saying in a low voice:

Pr. Blessed are you, Lord God of all creation,
for through your goodness we have received
the wine we offer you:
fruit of the vine and work of human hands,
it will become our spiritual drink.

If, however, the Offertory Chant is not sung, the Priest may speak these words aloud; at the end, the people may acclaim:

R. **Blessed be God for ever.**

The Priest completes additional personal preparatory rites, and THE PEOPLE STAND as he says:

Pr. Pray, brethren (brothers and sisters),
that my sacrifice and yours
may be acceptable to God,
the almighty Father.

The people reply:

R. **May the Lord accept the sacrifice at your hands**
for the praise and glory of his name,
for our good
and the good of all his holy Church.

The Prayer over the Offerings

The Priest says one of the following Prayers over the Offerings, at the end of which the people acclaim:

R. **Amen.**

Receive, we pray, O Lord,
the offering made on the occasion
of this sealing of the sacred bond of Marriage,
and, just as your goodness is its origin,
may your providence guide its course.
Through Christ our Lord.

Or:

Receive in your kindness, Lord,
the offerings we bring in gladness before you,
and in your fatherly love
watch over those you have joined in a sacramental covenant.
Through Christ our Lord.

Or:

Show favour to our supplications, O Lord,
and receive with a kindly countenance
the oblations we offer for these your servants,
joined now in a holy covenant,
that through these mysteries
they may be strengthened
in love for one another and for you.
Through Christ our Lord.

The Eucharistic Prayer

The Priest invites the people to lift their hearts to God:

V. The Lord be with you.　　R. And with your spir-it.

V. Lift up your hearts.　　R. We lift them up to the Lord.

V. Let us give thanks to the Lord our God.　　R. It is right and just.

Extending his hands, the Priest says:

Pr. The Lord be with you.

The people reply:

R. **And with your spirit.**

The Priest, raising his hands, continues:

Pr. Lift up your hearts.

The people:

R. **We lift them up to the Lord.**

The Priest, with hands extended, adds:

Pr. Let us give thanks to the Lord our God.

The people:

R. **It is right and just.**

The Priest continues with one of the following Prefaces:

A

Preface: The dignity of the marriage covenant.

It is truly right and just, our duty and our salvation,
always and everywhere to give you thanks,
Lord, holy Father, almighty and eternal God.

For you have forged the covenant of marriage
as a sweet yoke of harmony
and an unbreakable bond of peace,
so that the chaste and fruitful love of holy Matrimony
may serve to increase the children you adopt as your own.

By your providence and grace, O Lord,
you accomplish the wonder of this twofold design:
that, while the birth of children brings beauty to the world,
their rebirth in Baptism gives increase to the Church,
through Christ our Lord.

Through him, with the Angels and all the Saints,
we sing the hymn of your praise,
as without end we acclaim:

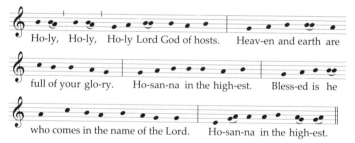

R. Holy, Holy, Holy Lord God of hosts.
Heaven and earth are full of your glory.
Hosanna in the highest.
Blessed is he who comes in the name of the Lord.
Hosanna in the highest.

After the singing of the Holy, Holy, Holy... THE PEOPLE KNEEL for
the remainder of the Eucharistic Prayer.

B

Preface: The great Sacrament of Matrimony.

It is truly right and just, our duty and our salvation,
always and everywhere to give you thanks,
Lord, holy Father, almighty and eternal God,
through Christ our Lord.

For in him you have made a new covenant with your people,
so that, as you have redeemed man and woman
by the mystery of Christ's Death and Resurrection,
so in Christ you might make them partakers of divine nature
and joint heirs with him of heavenly glory.

In the union of husband and wife
you give a sign of Christ's loving gift of grace,
so that the Sacrament we celebrate
might draw us back more deeply
into the wondrous design of your love.

And so, with the Angels and all the Saints,
we praise you, and without end we acclaim:

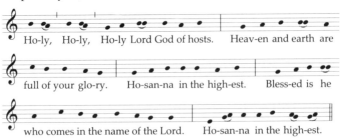

Ho-ly, Ho-ly, Ho-ly Lord God of hosts. Heav-en and earth are
full of your glo-ry. Ho-san-na in the high-est. Bless-ed is he
who comes in the name of the Lord. Ho-san-na in the high-est.

R. **Holy, Holy, Holy Lord God of hosts.**
Heaven and earth are full of your glory.
Hosanna in the highest.
Blessed is he who comes in the name of the Lord.
Hosanna in the highest.

After the singing of the **Holy, Holy, Holy**... THE PEOPLE KNEEL for
the remainder of the Eucharistic Prayer.

C

Preface: Matrimony as a sign of divine love.

It is truly right and just, our duty and our salvation,
always and everywhere to give you thanks,
Lord, holy Father, almighty and eternal God.

For you willed that the human race,
created by the gift of your goodness,
should be raised to such high dignity
that in the union of husband and wife
you might bestow a true image of your love.

For those you created out of charity
you call to the law of charity without ceasing
and grant them a share in your eternal charity.

And so, the Sacrament of holy Matrimony,
as the abiding sign of your own love,
consecrates the love of man and woman,
through Christ our Lord.

Through him, with the Angels and all the Saints,
we sing the hymn of your praise, as without end we acclaim:

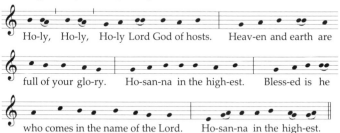

Ho-ly, Ho-ly, Ho-ly Lord God of hosts.   Heav-en and earth are

full of your glo-ry.   Ho-san-na in the high-est.   Bless-ed is he

who comes in the name of the Lord.   Ho-san-na in the high-est.

R. **Holy, Holy, Holy Lord God of hosts.**
Heaven and earth are full of your glory.
Hosanna in the highest.
Blessed is he who comes in the name of the Lord.
Hosanna in the highest.

After the singing of the **Holy, Holy, Holy**... THE PEOPLE KNEEL for
the remainder of the Eucharistic Prayer.

Texts for three of the principal Eucharistic Prayers follow.

In each of the Eucharistic Prayers a commemoration is made of the husband and wife.

Eucharistic Prayer I

(The Roman Canon)

Pr. To you, therefore, most merciful Father,
we make humble prayer and petition
through Jesus Christ, your Son, our Lord:
that you accept
and bless ✠ these gifts, these offerings,
these holy and unblemished sacrifices,
which we offer you firstly
for your holy catholic Church.
Be pleased to grant her peace,
to guard, unite and govern her
throughout the whole world,
together with your servant N. our Pope
and N. our Bishop,
and all those who, holding to the truth,
hand on the catholic and apostolic faith.

Commemoration of the Living.

Remember, Lord, your servants N. and N.
and all gathered here,
whose faith and devotion are known to you.
For them, we offer you this sacrifice of praise
or they offer it for themselves
and all who are dear to them:
for the redemption of their souls,
in hope of health and well-being,
and paying their homage to you,
the eternal God, living and true.

Within the Action.

In communion with those whose memory we venerate,
especially the glorious ever-Virgin Mary,
Mother of our God and Lord, Jesus Christ,
and blessed Joseph, her Spouse,
your blessed Apostles and Martyrs,
Peter and Paul, Andrew,
(James, John,
Thomas, James, Philip,
Bartholomew, Matthew,
Simon and Jude;
Linus, Cletus, Clement, Sixtus,
Cornelius, Cyprian,
Lawrence, Chrysogonus,
John and Paul,
Cosmas and Damian)
and all your Saints;
we ask that through their merits and prayers,
in all things we may be defended
by your protecting help.
(Through Christ our Lord. Amen.)

The proper form of the **Hanc igitur (Therefore, Lord, we pray)** is said.
The words in parentheses may be omitted, if the occasion so suggests:

Therefore, Lord, we pray:
graciously accept this oblation of our service,
the offering of your servants N. and N.
and of your whole family,
who entreat your majesty on their behalf;
and as you have brought them to their wedding day,
so (gladden them with your gift of the children they desire and)
bring them in your kindness
to the length of days for which they hope.
(Through Christ our Lord. Amen.)

Pr. Be pleased, O God, we pray,
to bless, acknowledge,
and approve this offering in every respect;
make it spiritual and acceptable,
so that it may become for us
the Body and Blood of your most beloved Son,
our Lord Jesus Christ.

On the day before he was to suffer,
he took bread in his holy and venerable hands,
and with eyes raised to heaven
to you, O God, his almighty Father,
giving you thanks, he said the blessing,
broke the bread
and gave it to his disciples, saying:

TAKE THIS, ALL OF YOU, AND EAT OF IT,
FOR THIS IS MY BODY,
WHICH WILL BE GIVEN UP FOR YOU.

He shows the consecrated host to the people, places it again on the paten, and genuflects in adoration.

In a similar way, when supper was ended,
he took this precious chalice
in his holy and venerable hands,
and once more giving you thanks, he said the blessing
and gave the chalice to his disciples, saying:

TAKE THIS, ALL OF YOU, AND DRINK FROM IT,
FOR THIS IS THE CHALICE OF MY BLOOD,
THE BLOOD OF THE NEW AND ETERNAL COVENANT,
WHICH WILL BE POURED OUT FOR YOU AND FOR MANY
FOR THE FORGIVENESS OF SINS.

DO THIS IN MEMORY OF ME.

He shows the chalice to the people, places it on the altar and genuflects in adoration.

Then he continues:

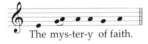
The mys-ter-y of faith.

Pr. The mystery of faith.

The people continue, acclaiming:

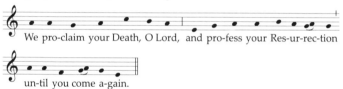

R. **We proclaim your Death, O Lord,**
and profess your Resurrection
until you come again.

Or:

R. **When we eat this Bread and drink this Cup,**
we proclaim your Death, O Lord,
until you come again.

Or:

R. **Save us, Saviour of the world,**
for by your Cross and Resurrection
you have set us free.

Then the Priest alone continues:

Pr. Therefore, O Lord,
as we celebrate the memorial of the blessed Passion,
the Resurrection from the dead,
and the glorious Ascension into heaven
of Christ, your Son, our Lord,
we, your servants and your holy people,
offer to your glorious majesty
from the gifts that you have given us,
this pure victim,
this holy victim,
this spotless victim,
the holy Bread of eternal life
and the Chalice of everlasting salvation.

Be pleased to look upon these offerings
with a serene and kindly countenance,
and to accept them,
as once you were pleased to accept
the gifts of your servant Abel the just,
the sacrifice of Abraham, our father in faith,
and the offering of your high priest Melchizedek,
a holy sacrifice, a spotless victim.

In humble prayer we ask you, almighty God:
command that these gifts be borne
by the hands of your holy Angel
to your altar on high
in the sight of your divine majesty,
so that all of us, who through this participation at the altar
receive the most holy Body and Blood of your Son,
may be filled with every grace and heavenly blessing.
(Through Christ our Lord. Amen.)

Commemoration of the Dead

Remember also, Lord, your servants N. and N.,
who have gone before us with the sign of faith
and rest in the sleep of peace.

Grant them, O Lord, we pray,
and all who sleep in Christ,
a place of refreshment, light and peace.
(Through Christ our Lord. Amen.)

To us, also, your servants, who, though sinners,
hope in your abundant mercies,
graciously grant some share
and fellowship with your holy Apostles and Martyrs:
with John the Baptist, Stephen,
Matthias, Barnabas,
(Ignatius, Alexander,
Marcellinus, Peter,
Felicity, Perpetua,
Agatha, Lucy,
Agnes, Cecilia, Anastasia)
and all your Saints;
admit us, we beseech you,
into their company,
not weighing our merits,
but granting us your pardon,
through Christ our Lord.

Through whom
you continue to make all these good things, O Lord;
you sanctify them, fill them with life,
bless them, and bestow them upon us.

The Priest takes the chalice and the paten with the host and, raising both, he says:

Through him, and with him, and in him,   O God, almighty Father,

in the unity of the Ho-ly Spir-it,   all glo-ry and hon-our is yours,

for ev - er and ev-er.   R. A-men.

Pr. Through him, and with him, and in him,
O God, almighty Father,
in the unity of the Holy Spirit,
all glory and honour is yours,
for ever and ever.

The people acclaim:

R. Amen.

Then follows the **Communion Rite**, p. 71.

Eucharistic Prayer II

Pr. You are indeed Holy, O Lord,
the fount of all holiness.

Make holy, therefore, these gifts, we pray,
by sending down your Spirit upon them like the dewfall,
so that they may become for us
the Body and ✠ Blood of our Lord, Jesus Christ.

At the time he was betrayed
and entered willingly into his Passion,
he took bread and, giving thanks, broke it,
and gave it to his disciples, saying:

> TAKE THIS, ALL OF YOU, AND EAT OF IT,
>
> FOR THIS IS MY BODY,
>
> WHICH WILL BE GIVEN UP FOR YOU.

He shows the consecrated host to the people, places it again on the paten, and genuflects in adoration.

In a similar way, when supper was ended,
he took the chalice
and, once more giving thanks,
he gave it to his disciples, saying:

> TAKE THIS, ALL OF YOU, AND DRINK FROM IT,
>
> FOR THIS IS THE CHALICE OF MY BLOOD,
>
> THE BLOOD OF THE NEW AND ETERNAL COVENANT,
>
> WHICH WILL BE POURED OUT FOR YOU AND FOR MANY
>
> FOR THE FORGIVENESS OF SINS.
>
> DO THIS IN MEMORY OF ME.

He shows the chalice to the people, places it on the altar and genuflects in adoration.

Then he continues:

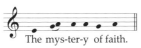
The mys-ter-y of faith.

Pr. The mystery of faith.

The people continue, acclaiming:

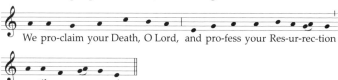

We pro-claim your Death, O Lord, and pro-fess your Res-ur-rec-tion un-til you come a-gain.

R. **We proclaim your Death, O Lord,**
and profess your Resurrection
until you come again.

Or:

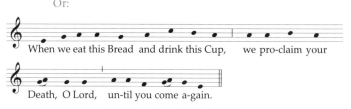

When we eat this Bread and drink this Cup, we pro-claim your Death, O Lord, un-til you come a-gain.

R. **When we eat this Bread and drink this Cup,**
we proclaim your Death, O Lord,
until you come again.

Or:

Save us, Sav-iour of the world, for by your Cross and Res-ur-rec-tion you have set us free.

R. **Save us, Saviour of the world,**
for by your Cross and Resurrection
you have set us free.

Then the Priest continues:

Pr. Therefore, as we celebrate
the memorial of his Death and Resurrection,
we offer you, Lord,
the Bread of life and the Chalice of salvation,
giving thanks that you have held us worthy
to be in your presence and minister to you.

Humbly we pray
that, partaking of the Body and Blood of Christ,
we may be gathered into one by the Holy Spirit.

Remember, Lord, your Church,
spread throughout the world,
and bring her to the fulness of charity,
together with N. our Pope and N. our Bishop
and all the clergy.
Be mindful also, Lord, of N. and N.,
whom you have brought to their wedding day,
so that by your grace
they may abide in mutual love and in peace.

Remember also our brothers and sisters
who have fallen asleep in the hope of the resurrection,
and all who have died in your mercy:
welcome them into the light of your face.
Have mercy on us all, we pray,
that with the Blessed Virgin Mary, Mother of God,
with blessed Joseph, her Spouse,
with the blessed Apostles,
and all the Saints who have pleased you throughout the ages,
we may merit to be coheirs to eternal life,
and may praise and glorify you

He joins his hands.

through your Son, Jesus Christ.

The Priest takes the chalice and the paten with the host and, raising both, he says:

Through him, and with him, and in him,   O God, almighty Father,
in the unity of the Ho-ly Spir-it,   all glo-ry and hon-our is yours,
for ev - er and ev-er.   R. A-men.

Pr. Through him, and with him, and in him,
O God, almighty Father,
in the unity of the Holy Spirit,
all glory and honour is yours,
for ever and ever.

The people acclaim:

R. Amen.

Then follows the **Communion Rite**, p. 71.

Eucharistic Prayer III

The Priest says:

Pr. You are indeed Holy, O Lord,
and all you have created
rightly gives you praise,
for through your Son our Lord Jesus Christ,
by the power and working of the Holy Spirit,
you give life to all things and make them holy,
and you never cease to gather a people to yourself,
so that from the rising of the sun to its setting
a pure sacrifice may be offered to your name.

Therefore, O Lord, we humbly implore you:
by the same Spirit graciously make holy
these gifts we have brought to you for consecration,
that they may become the Body and ✠ Blood
of your Son our Lord Jesus Christ,
at whose command we celebrate these mysteries.

For on the night he was betrayed
he himself took bread,
and, giving you thanks, he said the blessing,
broke the bread and gave it to his disciples, saying:

TAKE THIS, ALL OF YOU, AND EAT OF IT,
FOR THIS IS MY BODY,
WHICH WILL BE GIVEN UP FOR YOU.

He shows the consecrated host to the people, places it again on the paten, and genuflects in adoration.

In a similar way, when supper was ended,
he took the chalice,
and, giving you thanks, he said the blessing,
and gave the chalice to his disciples, saying:

TAKE THIS, ALL OF YOU, AND DRINK FROM IT,
FOR THIS IS THE CHALICE OF MY BLOOD,
THE BLOOD OF THE NEW AND ETERNAL COVENANT,
WHICH WILL BE POURED OUT FOR YOU AND FOR MANY
FOR THE FORGIVENESS OF SINS.
DO THIS IN MEMORY OF ME.

He shows the chalice to the people, places it on the altar and genuflects in adoration.

Then he continues:

The mys-ter-y of faith.

Pr. The mystery of faith.

The people continue, acclaiming:

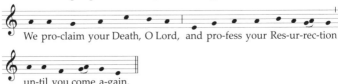

We pro-claim your Death, O Lord, and pro-fess your Res-ur-rec-tion

un-til you come a-gain.

R. **We proclaim your Death, O Lord,
and profess your Resurrection
until you come again.**

Or:

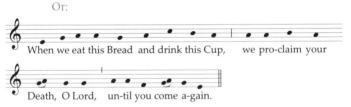

When we eat this Bread and drink this Cup, we pro-claim your

Death, O Lord, un-til you come a-gain.

R. **When we eat this Bread and drink this Cup,
we proclaim your Death, O Lord,
until you come again.**

Or:

Save us, Sav-iour of the world, for by your Cross and Res-ur-rec-tion

you have set us free.

R. **Save us, Saviour of the world,
for by your Cross and Resurrection
you have set us free.**

The Priest continues:

Pr. Therefore, O Lord, as we celebrate the memorial
of the saving Passion of your Son,
his wondrous Resurrection
and Ascension into heaven,
and as we look forward to his second coming,
we offer you in thanksgiving
this holy and living sacrifice.

Look, we pray, upon the oblation of your Church
and, recognizing the sacrificial Victim by whose death
you willed to reconcile us to yourself,
grant that we, who are nourished
by the Body and Blood of your Son
and filled with his Holy Spirit,
may become one body, one spirit in Christ.

May he make of us
an eternal offering to you,
so that we may obtain an inheritance with your elect,
especially with the most Blessed Virgin Mary, Mother of God,
with blessed Joseph, her Spouse,
with your blessed Apostles and glorious Martyrs
(with Saint N.: *the Saint of the day or Patron Saint*)
and with all the Saints,
on whose constant intercession in your presence
we rely for unfailing help.

May this Sacrifice of our reconciliation,
we pray, O Lord,
advance the peace and salvation of all the world.
Be pleased to confirm in faith and charity
your pilgrim Church on earth,
with your servant N. our Pope and N. our Bishop,
the Order of Bishops, all the clergy,
and the entire people you have gained for your own.
Listen graciously to the prayers of this family,
whom you have summoned before you.

Strengthen, we pray, in the grace of Marriage N. and N.,
whom you have brought happily to their wedding day,
that under your protection
they may always be faithful in their lives
to the covenant they have sealed in your presence.
In your compassion, O merciful Father,
gather to yourself all your children
scattered throughout the world.

To our departed brothers and sisters
and to all who were pleasing to you
at their passing from this life,
give kind admittance to your kingdom.
There we hope to enjoy for ever the fullness of your glory
through Christ our Lord,
through whom you bestow on the world all that is good.

*The Priest takes the chalice and the paten with the host and,
raising both, he says:*

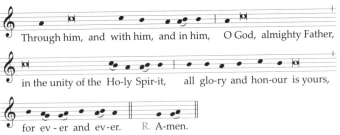

Through him, and with him, and in him,   O God, almighty Father,
in the unity of the Ho-ly Spir-it,   all glo-ry and hon-our is yours,
for ev - er and ev-er.   R. A-men.

Pr. Through him, and with him, and in him,
O God, almighty Father,
in the unity of the Holy Spirit,
all glory and honour is yours,
for ever and ever.

The people acclaim:

R. **Amen.**

Then follows the **Communion Rite.**

The Communion Rite

The Lord's Prayer

After the chalice and paten have been set down, THE PEOPLE STAND and the Priest says:

Pr. At the Saviour's command
and formed by divine teaching,
we dare to say:

Together with the people, he continues:

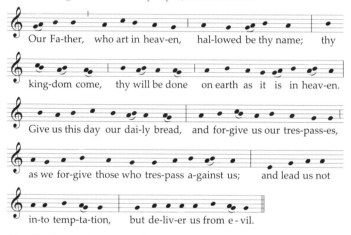

Our Father, who art in heaven,
hallowed be thy name;
thy kingdom come,
thy will be done
on earth as it is in heaven.
Give us this day our daily bread,
and forgive us our trespasses,
as we forgive those who trespass against us;
and lead us not into temptation,
but deliver us from evil.

Or:

Pa-ter nos-ter, qui es in cae-lis: san-cti-fi-cé-tur no-men tu-um;

ad-vé-ni-at reg-num tu-um; fi-at vo-lún-tas tu-a, si-cut in cae-lo,

et in ter-ra. Pa-nem nos-trum co-ti-di-á-num da no-bis hó-di-e;

et di-mít-te no-bis dé-bi-ta nos-tra, si-cut et nos di-mít-ti-mus

de-bi-tó-ri-bus nos-tris; et ne nos in-dú-cas in ten-ta-ti - ó-nem;

sed lí-be-ra nos a ma-lo.

Nuptial Blessing

After the **Our Father**, the prayer **Deliver us** is omitted. The Priest, standing and facing the bride and bridegroom, invokes upon them God's blessing, and this is never omitted.

In the invitation, if one or both of the spouses will not be receiving Communion, the words in parentheses are omitted. In the prayer, the words in parentheses may be omitted if it seems that circumstances suggest it, for example, if the bride and bridegroom are advanced in years.

The bride and bridegroom approach the altar or, if appropriate, they remain at their place and kneel. The Priest, with hands joined, calls upon those present to pray:

Dear brothers and sisters,
let us humbly pray to the Lord
that on these his servants, now married in Christ,
he may mercifully pour out
the blessing of his grace
and make of one heart in love
(by the Sacrament of Christ's Body and Blood)
those he has joined by a holy covenant.

Or:

Now let us humbly invoke God's blessing
upon this bride and groom,
that in his kindness he may favour with his help
those on whom he has bestowed the Sacrament
    of Matrimony.

Or:

Let us pray to the Lord for this bride and groom,
who come to the altar as they begin their married life,
that (partaking of the Body and Blood of Christ)
they may always be bound together by love
    for one another.

Or:

Let us humbly invoke by our prayers,
    dear brothers and sisters,
God's blessing upon this bride and groom,
that in his kindness he may favour with his help
those on whom he has bestowed
    the Sacrament of Matrimony.

And all pray in silence for a while.

O God, who by your mighty power
created all things out of nothing,
and, when you had set in place
the beginnings of the universe,
formed man and woman in your own image,
making the woman an inseparable helpmate to the man,
that they might no longer be two, but one flesh,
and taught that what you were pleased to make one
must never be divided;

O God, who consecrated the bond of Marriage
by so great a mystery
that in the wedding covenant you foreshadowed
the Sacrament of Christ and his Church;

O God, by whom woman is joined to man
and the companionship they had in the beginning
is endowed with the one blessing
not forfeited by original sin
nor washed away by the flood.

Look now with favour on these your servants,
joined together in Marriage,
who ask to be strengthened by your blessing.
Send down on them the grace of the Holy Spirit
and pour your love into their hearts,
that they may remain faithful
    in the Marriage covenant.

May the grace of love and peace
abide in your daughter N.,
and let her always follow the example
    of those holy women
whose praises are sung in the Scriptures.

May her husband entrust his heart to her,
so that, acknowledging her as his equal
and his joint heir to the life of grace,

he may show her due honour
and cherish her always
with the love that Christ has for his Church.

And now, Lord, we implore you:
may these your servants
hold fast to the faith and keep your commandments;
made one in the flesh,
may they be blameless in all they do;
and with the strength that comes from the Gospel,
may they bear true witness to Christ before all;
(may they be blessed with children,
and prove themselves virtuous parents,
who live to see their children's children).

And grant that,
reaching at last together the fullness of years
for which they hope,
they may come to the life of the blessed
in the Kingdom of Heaven.
Through Christ our Lord.
R. **Amen.**

Or:

Holy Father,
who formed man in your own image,
male and female you created them,
so that as husband and wife, united in body and heart,
they might fulfil their calling in the world;

O God, who, to reveal the great design you formed
    in your love,
willed that the love of spouses for each other
should foreshadow the covenant you graciously made
    with your people,
so that, by fulfilment of the sacramental sign,
the mystical marriage of Christ with his Church
might become manifest
in the union of husband and wife among your faithful;

Graciously stretch out your right hand
over these your servants (N. and N.), we pray,
and pour into their hearts the power of the Holy Spirit.

Grant, O Lord,
that, as they enter upon this sacramental union,
they may share with one another the gifts of your love
and, by being for each other a sign of your presence,
become one heart and one mind.

May they also sustain, O Lord, by their deeds
the home they are forming
(and prepare their children
to become members of your heavenly household
by raising them in the way of the Gospel).

Graciously crown with your blessings your daughter N.,
so that, by being a good wife (and mother),
she may bring warmth to her home with a love that is pure
and adorn it with welcoming graciousness.

Bestow a heavenly blessing also, O Lord,
on N., your servant,
that he may be a worthy, good and
faithful husband (and a provident father).

Grant, holy Father,
that, desiring to approach your table
as a couple joined in Marriage in your presence,
they may one day have the joy
of taking part in your great banquet in heaven.
Through Christ our Lord.
R. **Amen.**

Or:

Holy Father, maker of the whole world,
who created man and woman in your own image
and willed that their union be crowned with your blessing,
we humbly beseech you for these your servants,
who are joined today in the Sacrament of Matrimony.

May your abundant blessing, Lord,
come down upon this bride, N.,
and upon N., her companion for life,
and may the power of your Holy Spirit
set their hearts aflame from on high,
so that, living out together the gift of Matrimony,
they may (adorn their family with children
    and) enrich the Church.

In happiness may they praise you, O Lord,
in sorrow may they seek you out;
may they have the joy of your presence
to assist them in their toil,
and know that you are near
to comfort them in their need;
let them pray to you in the holy assembly
and bear witness to you in the world,
and after a happy old age,
together with the circle of friends that surrounds them,
may they come to the Kingdom of Heaven.
Through Christ our Lord.
R. **Amen.**

> If the marriage takes place without a Eucharist then the
> Minister immediately blesses the people, saying:

May almighty God bless all of you,
    who are gathered here,
the Father, and the Son, ✠ and the Holy Spirit.
R. **Amen.**

The Peace

Pr. The peace of the Lord be with you always.

The people reply:

R. And with your spirit.

Then the Deacon, or the Priest, adds:

Pr. Let us offer each other the sign of peace.

Then the bride and bridegroom and all present offer one another a sign, in keeping with local customs, that expresses peace, communion and charity.

Breaking of the Bread

Sharing in the body and blood of our Saviour by receiving Holy Communion is a mark of the fulness of Christian unity. This is why only those who are already in the communion of the Roman Catholic Church receive this Sacrament.

Then the Priest takes the host, breaks it over the paten, and places a small piece in the chalice, saying quietly:

Pr. May this mingling of the Body and Blood
of our Lord Jesus Christ
bring eternal life to us who receive it.

Meanwhile the following is sung or said:

Lamb of God, * you take a-way the sins of the world,

have mer-cy on us.

Lamb of God, * you take a-way the sins of the world,

have mer-cy on us.

Lamb of God, * you take a-way the sins of the world,

grant us peace.

**Lamb of God, you take away the sins of the world,
have mercy on us.
Lamb of God, you take away the sins of the world,
have mercy on us.
Lamb of God, you take away the sins of the world,
grant us peace.**

Or:

A-gnus De - i, * qui tol-lis pec-cá-ta mun-di: mi-se-ré-re no-bis.

A-gnus De - i, * qui tol-lis pec-cá-ta mun-di: mi-se-ré-re no-bis.

A-gnus De - i, * qui tol-lis pec-cá-ta mun-di: do-na no-bis pa-cem.

The invocation may even be repeated several times if the fraction is prolonged. Only the final time, however, is **grant us peace** said. After the Lamb of God, THE PEOPLE KNEEL.

Invitation to Communion

After his private prayers of preparation the Priest genuflects, takes the host and, holding it slightly raised above the paten or above the chalice says aloud:

Pr. Behold the Lamb of God,
behold him who takes away the sins of the world.
Blessed are those called to the supper of the Lamb.

And together with the people he adds once:

R. Lord, I am not worthy
that you should enter under my roof,
but only say the word
and my soul shall be healed.

While the Priest is receiving the Body of Christ, the Communion Chant begins.

Communion Procession

After the Priest has reverently consumed the Body and Blood of Christ he takes the paten or ciborium and approaches the communicants. The Priest raises a host slightly and shows it to each of the communicants, saying:

Pr. The Body of Christ.

The communicant replies:

R. Amen.

And receives Holy Communion.

When Communion is ministered from the chalice the minister of the chalice raises it slightly and shows it to each of the communicants, saying:

Pr. The Blood of Christ.

The communicant replies:

R. **Amen.**

And receives Holy Communion.

The Communion Antiphon may be sung or said during communion. There are three choices:

Cf. Eph 5:25,27

Christ loved the Church and handed himself over for her,
to present her as a holy and spotless bride for himself
(E.T. alleluia).

Or:

Jn 13:34

I give you a new commandment, that you love one another
as I have loved you, says the Lord (E.T. alleluia).

Or:

Ps 33:2,9

I will bless the Lord at all times,
praise of him is always in my mouth.
Taste and see that the Lord is good;
blessed the man who seeks refuge in him (E.T. alleluia).

After the distribution of Communion THE PEOPLE SIT and, if appropriate, a sacred silence may be observed for a while, or a psalm or other canticle of praise or a hymn may be sung.

Prayer after Communion

Then, the Priest says:

Pr. Let us pray.

ALL STAND and pray in silence for a while, unless silence has just been observed. Then the Priest says one of the following the Prayers after Communion, at the end of which the people acclaim:

R. Amen.

By the power of this sacrifice, O Lord,
accompany with your loving favour
what in your providence you have instituted,
so as to make of one heart in love
those you have already joined in this holy union
(and replenished with the one Bread and the one Chalice).
Through Christ our Lord.

Or:

Having been made partakers at your table,
we pray, O Lord,
that those who are united by the Sacrament of Marriage
may always hold fast to you
and proclaim your name to the world.
Through Christ our Lord.

Or:

Grant, we pray, almighty God,
that the power of the Sacrament we have received
may find growth in these your servants
and that the effects of the sacrifice we have offered
may be felt by us all.
Through Christ our Lord.

The Concluding Rites

Solemn Blessing

The Priest says:

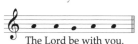
The Lord be with you.

Pr. The Lord be with you.

The people reply:

And with your spir-it.

R. **And with your spirit.**

The Deacon, or in his absence, the Priest himself says:

Bow down for the bless-ing.

Pr. Bow down for the blessing.

A

The Priest, with hands extended over the bride and bridegroom, says:

May God the eternal Father
keep you of one heart in love for one another,
that the peace of Christ may dwell in you
and abide always in your home.

R. **Amen.**

May you be blessed in your children,
have solace in your friends
and enjoy true peace with everyone.

R. **Amen.**

May you be witnesses in the world to God's charity,
so that the afflicted and needy who have known your kindness
may one day receive you thankfully
into the eternal dwelling of God.

R. **Amen.**

And he blesses all the people, adding:

And may almighty God bless all of you, who are gathered here, the Father, and the Son, ✠ and the Holy Spirit.

R. **Amen.**

B

The Priest, with hands extended over the bride and bridegroom, says:

May God the all-powerful Father grant you his joy and bless you in your children.

R. **Amen.**

May the Only Begotten Son of God stand by you with compassion in good times and in bad.

R. **Amen.**

May the Holy Spirit of God always pour forth his love into your hearts.

R. **Amen.**

And he blesses all the people, adding:

And may almighty God bless all of you, who are gathered here, the Father, and the Son, ✠ and the Holy Spirit.

R. **Amen.**

C

The Priest, with hands extended over the bride and bridegroom, says:

May the Lord Jesus, who graced the marriage at Cana by his presence, bless you and your loved ones.

R. **Amen.**

May he, who loved the Church to the end, unceasingly pour his love into your hearts.

R. **Amen.**

May the Lord grant that, bearing witness to faith in his Resurrection, you may await with joy the blessed hope to come.

R. **Amen.**

And he blesses all the people, adding:

And may almighty God bless all of you, who are gathered here, the Father, and the Son, ✠ and the Holy Spirit.

R. **Amen.**

Then the Deacon, or the Priest himself, says the Dismissal, to which in all cases the people reply: **Thanks be to God.**

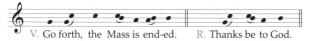
V. Go forth, the Mass is end-ed.   R. Thanks be to God.

Pr. Go forth, the Mass is ended.

Or:

V. Go and an-nounce the Gos-pel of the Lord.   R. Thanks be to God.

Pr. Go and announce the Gospel of the Lord.

Or:

V. Go in peace, glorifying the Lord by your life.   R. Thanks be to God.

Pr. Go in peace, glorifying the Lord by your life.

Or:

V. Go in peace.   R. Thanks be to God.

Pr. Go in peace.

When the Mass is concluded, the newly married couple, the witnesses and the Priest sign the Marriage record. The signing may be done in the vesting room or in the presence of the people; however it is not to be done on the altar.